NOTED NAMES FOR ARMENIAN BABY BOYS AND GIRLS

AHSRAH AYIR

Made with ♥ on the Notion Press Platform
www.notionpress.com

Contents

Contents

Preface

Experts say that the name has a great impact on the life of a human being, so the name should be meaningful. Therefore, while naming a child, parents insist that the name be auspicious and reflect the personality of the child well. According to the principles of naming, it is concluded that the name has a special relationship with our behavior. Names in our lives not only give information about our personality, but they are also an important part of our future.

If seen, the first identity of a child is his or her name, which remains associated with him or her throughout his or her life. There are many things to keep in mind while naming a child, such as family customs, traditions, social rules, and many more. All these aspects should be considered while choosing a name. The name should be chosen so that it is easy to pronounce as well as meaningful.

In many places, you can guess the religion of the child by his name. By the way, in modern times, people do not give much importance to religions, etc. when naming. All they need is a catchy and easy name for their babies. Despite all these things, it is difficult for any parent to name a child because every parent wants their child's name to be the most different and attractive.

Generally, a baby should be named in such a way that it is sweet and beautiful to hear. Too difficult a name can sometimes cause trouble for that child in the future. Often, there are mistakes in the documents made while writing difficult names, which have to be circulated to the government offices to correct them, and many problems have to be faced. So the name should be something that is beautiful as well as easy to speak and write. This will save you and your baby from many problems.

If you take care of the things mentioned here, then you will be able to choose the best name for your baby.

Keep in mind that trendy names should be avoided. Choose a simple name that has a deep message or meaning hidden in it. Nowadays, the trend of naming such names has increased a lot. At the same time, it is believed that the meaning of the name also affects the nature of people. So, whatever name you give, its meaning will affect the behaviour of your child. Having the name for too long can upset the child. Give names that are easy to pronounce. The spelling of the name should also be easy.

In the end, we can say that naming babies is a very important and difficult task. Even before the birth of the child, parents spend a lot of time thinking about the name of the child, and sometimes even after the birth of the child, no name is finalized. In such a situation, keeping in mind the above-mentioned tips, you can give the right name to your child, and this book can prove to be helpful in this. It consists of alphabetically chosen and meaningful names for your baby. So it can become a useful and collectible book for you, your family, and your friends.

—Author

CHAPTER ONE

Armenian Baby Names—A

Abaven—(m)—protector

Abel—(m)—breathe

Abirad—(m)—miserable

Abril—(f)—to live, month of april

Acher—(m)—eyes

Adela—(f)—pleasant, noble

Adele—(f)—noble

Adelisa—(f)—of the nobility noble

Ademir—(m)—noble protector

Adis—(m)—good news, saint

Ado—(m)—royal word

Adolf—(m)—noble wolf

Adom—(m)—help from god

Adour—(m)—gift from god, given from god

Adriana—(f)—coming from city

Adrig—(m)—god gift

Adrine—(f)—citizen, of the adriatic sea

Adroushan—(m)—temple, devoted to fire worship

Aghakhin—(f)—servant

Aghan—(m)—head of troop

Aghasi—(m)—head of troop
Aghavni—(f)—dove, pigeon
Aghavni—(f)—pigeon
Aghavnig—(f)—dove-small
Agheg—(m)—good, well, kind
Agheksanter—(m)—protector
Aghounig—(f)—dove
Aghpiur—(f)—source
Aghpourig—(f)—source
Aghvor—(f)—beautiful
Agner—(f)—diamonds, chaste, pure, holy
Agourig—(f)—little axe
Agustina—(f)—majestic, grand
Aharon—(m)—lofty, exalted, high mountain
Ahmet—(m)—highly praised, thanks god
Aicha—(f)—life
Aida—(f)—happy, famous, prosperous
Aidzemnig—(f)—young goat
Aidziam—(f)—young goat
Aidzig—(f)—goat, small
Aik—(f)—dawn, daybreak, morning
Aiki—(f)—vineyard
Aikoun—(f)—dawn
Aina—(f)—love, affection vegetables, greens
Aira—(m)—pious, clear
Ajla—(f)—kind, soft
Akabe—(f)—jewel of the sea
Akabi—(f)—jewel of the sea, love
Aknes—(f)—chaste
Alabina—(f)—kind, soft
Alan—(m)—god of shine, handsome, cheerful, rock
Alban—(m)—white
Albert—(m)—beautifully, noble behaviour

Aldijan—(m)—daring, winner
Aldijana—(f)—kind, soft
Aldin—(m)—old friend
Alec—(m)—protector
Aleena—(f)—noble
Alen—(m)—noble behaviour
Aleni—(f)—mermaid
Alenoush—(f)—sweet, white wave
Alexa—(f)—helper, defender
Alexan—(m)—protector
Alexander—(m)—guardian
Alexandra—(f)—defender
Alfred—(m)—he gets that board of elves
Alice—(f)—of noble kind, of the nobility
Alicia—(f)—of noble birth
Alicio—(m)—virtuous
Alids—(f)—gentle
Alids—(f)—kind
Alidz—(f)—joyous, merry, gentle
Alik—(f)—wave of the ocean
Alik—(m)—wave
Aliki—(f)—honest
Alin—(f)—soothe, to soothe, bearer of the light
Alin—(m)—fair, handsome
Alina—(f)—noble
Aline—(f)—bearer or transporter of light, to soothe
Alis—(f)—of noble kind
Alisa—(f)—noble, nobility, of noble kind
Alisia—(f)—gentle
Alix—(f)—noble
Alma—(f)—girl
Almasd—(f)—diamond
Almast—(f)—diamond

Almeida—(f)—kind, soft

Almina—(f)—kind, soft

Almut—(f)—of noble spirit

Alois—(m)—famous

Aloys—(m)—sun

Alvart—(f)—red rose

Alyag—(f)—small wave

Alyce—(f)—of the nobility

Amalia—(f)—industrious one

Amar—(m)—summer

Amara—(f)—imperishable

Amaryllis—(f)—sparkling

Amas—(m)—force of god

Amasia—(f)—rural community

Amelie—(f)—hard working, industrious, striving

Amour—(m)—tight, solid, strong, firm

Ampagoum—(m)—rare

Ana elena—(f)—kind, soft

Ana livia—(f)—kind, soft

Anag—(m)—illuminator, very handsome

Anahid—(f)—the immaculate, divine, the moon goddess

Anais—(f)—the immaculate, divine

Anania—(m)—whom lord covers or protects

Ananoun—(m)—having no name

Anas—(m)—friendly, neighbour, friendly

Anastas—(m)—resurrection, springtime

Anastasia—(f)—risen by baptism to new life

Anayis—(f)—the immaculate

Anca—(f)—armenian national committee of america

Andar—(m)—forest

Anderson—(m)—son

Andertjosef—(m)—daring, winner

Andon—(m)—flower, colour, invaluable

Andranik—(m)—the first

Andrea—(f)—manlike, manly, brave

Andreas—(m)—manlike, manly, brave

Andrei—(m)—manlike

Angela—(f)—angel

Angelika—(f)—like an angel

Angely—(f)—kind, soft

Ani—(f)—ancient capital of Armenia, grace, favour, ancient city

Aniela—(f)—angel

Anig—(f)—a diminutive of ani

Anika—(f)—soft nature

Anita—(f)—gracious

Ankhosig—(f)—quiet

Ankine—(f)—priceless, valuable, precious

Anna—(f)—grace, favour of god, present, graceful

Annabel—(f)—gracious

Annamaria—(f)—grace

Annemarie—(f)—gracious

Annman—(f)—unequalled

Annuman—(f)—unequalled

Ano—(f)—awe, reverence, goddess of armenian mythology representing family and fertility

Anoush—(f)—sweet, sweetness

Anoushavan—(m)—dedicated to the forest of sosi, sweet village

Anoushig—(f)—pretty, sweet, sweetness

Antaram—(f)—eternal flower, evergreen, unfading

Anti—(m)—grand, oldest member, usually referring to the first born son

Antigona—(f)—kind, soft

Anto—(m)—grand, oldest member, usually referring to the first born son

Antonella—(f)—praiseworthy

Antonia—(f)—highly, praise worthy

Antranig—(m)—first born son, grand, oldest member

Antreas—(m)—grand, oldest member, usually referring to the first born son

Antrias—(m)—man of courage

Antsrev—(f)—rain

Antsrev—(f)—rain

Antsrev—(m)—rain

Antsrevig—(f)—small rain

Anuja—(f)—youthful, young at heart

Anush—(f)—single, sweet, nice

Apas—(m)—from arabic austere

Apel—(m)—breathe

Apisoghom—(m)—father of peace

Apkar—(m)—king

Apov—(m)—assured by hope of god

Apraham—(m)—father of many

Ara—(m)—armenian mythological name which symbolizes the spring, bringer of productivity, swift, king, embellishing, adorning

Araa—(m)—opinion

Arad—(m)—abundant

Arakadz—(m)—a mountain in armenia, throne of armenia

Arakel—(m)—disciple of jesus, send through a messenger, to send

Arakil—(f)—stork, the bird

Araks—(f)—arax river

Araksi—(f)—river

Aram—(m)—high, exalted, ancestor, quiet, the father of ara keghetsig, excellency or highness

Aramais—(m)—gift of god ara

Aramaniag—(m)—adorning collar

Aramayis—(m)—armenian mythological name, mild, sweet, gift of god ara

Aramazt—(m)—father of armenian gods, symbol for fertility

Arameh—(m)—Excellency, highness, the father of ara keghetsig

Aramig—(m)—the father of ara keghetsig, excellency or highness

Aramouhi—(f)—high, exalted, ancestor feminine

Aran—(m)—elbow, righteous

Arantsar—(m)—martyr, prince, war

Arapo—(m)—hero

Ararad—(m)—mountain ararad

Ararat—(m)—mount ararat, traditional armenian name

Arax—(f)—a river in armenia, daughter of a king

Araxia—(f)—variation of arax, river that inspires poetic talent

Araz—(f)—arax river, the name of a river in armenia

Archoug—(m)—bear cub

Arda—(f)—grand daughter of roupen, ideal, perfect

Arda—(m)—ideal, perfect

Ardag—(m)—ideal, perfect

Ardahan—(m)—city in ancient armenia

Ardanoush—(f)—perfect+sweet

Ardash—(m)—prince of justce

Ardashad—(m)—descendant of the joyous light

Ardashes—(m)—just ruler, prince of justice

Ardavan—(m)—perfect village

Ardavan—(m)—protector of righteousness

Ardavazt—(m)—honest ruler

Ardem—(m)—healthy

Ardemis—(f)— healthy

Ardouyd—(f)—skylark

Ardsat—(m)—silver

Ardziv—(m)—eagle

Ardzroun—(m)—noble armenian family

Ardzvi—(f)—eagle

Ardzvig—(f)—eagle

Ared—(m)—asteroid

Areen—(f)—assumed to be from arun meaning blood

Arek—(m)—lofty, exalted, high mountain, sun, the 8th armenian month, beam of light

Arekag—(m)—sun

Arekag—(m)—sun god in armenian mythology

Areknaz—(f)—sun+caprice

Areknazan—(f)—sun+caprice

Aren—(m)—eagle, ruler, peace, gift from god, a city in armenia

Areni—(f)—a village in armenia famous for it's wine

Arev—(f)—sun

Arevalous—(f)—sunlight

Arevhad—(f)—sun+grain

Arevig—(f)—like the sun

Arevshad—(m)—full of sun, long life, in eternal sun

Argishd—(m)—name of an ancient armenian king

Ari—(m)—lion, brave, inner skin, eagle

Arin—(f)—a village in Armenia, assumed to be from arun meaning blood

Arine—(f)—brave female

Arineh—(f)—brave woman

Aris—(m)—river

Arisdages—(m)—the best, name of king

Arka—(m)—king

Arkam—(m)—generous, king's son

Arkina—(f)—invaluable, priceless, a small city or district in medieval armenia located near ani

Arkishdi—(m)—urartian king

Arlen—(m)—from irish pledge

Arman—(m)—Armenian, longing, wish, hope, desire, man in the army

Armani—(f)—armenian woman, mountain in Armenia, free woman

Armani—(m)—freeman

Armanoush—(f)—daughter of armen

Armaveni—(f)—tree

Armavir—(m)—first capital of armenia

Armen—(m)—armenian, high place, castle, palace, derived from the armenian, mythological name, head of armenian race

Armenag—(m)—armenian

Armenag—(m)—derived from the armenian, mythological name, head of armenian race

Armenak—(m)—armenian

Armeni—(m)—derived from the armenian, mythological name, head of armenian race

Armenig—(f)—armenian

Armenouhi—(f)—armenian lady, from armenia, feminine of armen

Armenouhie—(f)—woman from armenia

Armig—(m)—derived from the armenian, mythological name, head of armenian race

Armine—(f)—Armenian, modern feminine variant of armen

Armineh—(f)—desire, goal

Armo—(m)—derived from the armenian, mythological name, head of armenian race

Arnag—(m)—a man with strength and high energy, virile, war

Arnel—(m)—daring, winner

Arno—(m)—singer, lofty, exalted

Aro—(m)—derived from the armenian, mythological name, head of armenian race

Arous—(f)—short for arousiag

Arousiag—(f)—venus, shining, light emiting

Arousyag—(f)—morning star, venus

Arpa—(f)—a river in armenia

Arpag—(m)—source of sun

Arpeni—(f)—fancy name for the sun, modern varian for arpi

Arpi—(f)—sun, sunshine, the rising sun

Arpiar—(m)—man of light, sunny

Arpig—(f)—the rising sun

Arpina—(f)—rising of sun

Arpine—(f)—sun, the name of a village in armenia

Arpineh—(f)—sun

Arpoun—(m)—real force, sunny

Arra—(m)—pious, clear

Arsen—(m)—indo european bear, virile male, potent, strong

Arshag—(m)—bear's cup, messenger of heaven, heir to the throne

Arshaganoush—(f)—sweet bear's cup, messenger of heaven

Arshagouhi—(f)—heiress to throne

Arshalooys—(f)—dawn, sunrise

Arshalous—(m)—dawn

Arshalouys—(m)—dawn

Arsham—(m)—bear strong, very strong
Arshavir—(m)—to rush, invade, attack
Arshen—(m)—from the bear
Arshig—(f)—dawn
Arsho—(f)—dawn
Arsho—(f)—diminutive of arsahalooys, dawn
Arsine—(f)—female bear, feminine of arsen
Artar—(m)—just, fair
Artashes—(m)—founder of artaxiad dynasty
Artaxes—(m)—founder of artaxiad dynasty
Artaxiad—(m)—name of a king
Artaxias—(m)—founder of artaxiad dynasty
Arti—(m)—modern, of the times
Artik—(m)—a city in armenia's shirak province
Artoon—(m)—awake, alert
Artoun—(m)—awake
Artsan—(m)—statue
Artsvi—(m)—of an eagle, wings of an eagle
Artzouig—(f)—eaglet
Arudz—(m)—lion
Arus—(f)—light emiting
Arwen—(f)—royal maiden
Ary—(m)—dull black, dark
Arzouman—(m)—desirable man
Asadoor—(m)—given by god
Asadour—(m)—given to god, most prosperous one
Asbed—(m)—knight
Asbourag—(m)—flying star
Asdghig—(f)—small star, armenian goddess corresponding to venus
Asdig—(f)—little star
Asdvadzadour—(m)—god-given
Asghig—(f)—little star

Ashken—(f)—on of the queens of ancient armenia

Ashkhen—(f)—earthly

Ashod—(m)—armenian king, founder of the pakradouni dynasty, world, planet

Ashot—(m)—pious, clear

Ashoun—(f)—autumn, fall

Ashrina—(f)—kind, soft

Asima—(f)—defender

Asisa—(f)—ripe

Askanaz—(m)—rimy flames

Askdorci—(f)—kind, soft

Asmin—(f)—god's gift, jasmine

Astine—(f)—the beautiful

Astrid—(f)—divine beauty, strength

Atam—(m)—adam, self, spiritual, man

Atanas—(m)—immortal, resurrection

Atapeg—(m)—senior

Atef—(m)—the kind one

Athangelos—(m)—name of a historian

Atreo—(m)—daring, winner

Auriel—(m)—lion of god

Aurora—(f)—gold

Aus—(m)—to give gift

Avak—(m)—great, the first, senior

Avarair—(m)—pious, clear

Avarayr—(m)—region in armenia

Aved—(m)—goog news

Avedig—(m)—good tidings

Avedis—(m)—brings good news, good tidings

Avig—(m)—good news

Avo—(m)—good news

Aya—(f)—sign

Ayden—(m)—little

Ayk—(m)—dawn
Ayse—(f)—kind, soft
Azad—(m)—liberated
Azadig—(f)—feminine of azad, free, independent
Azadouhi—(f)—free woman, female
Azaduhi—(f)—free, independent
Azaria—(m)—god has helped
Azat—(m)—gazelle
Azkanoush—(f)—sweet
Aznavour—(m)—giant man, titan, hero
Azniv—(f)—gentle, kind
Azusa—(f)—water lily

CHAPTER TWO

ARMENIAN BABY NAMES—B

Bab—(m)—door, gate entrance, gateway, grandfather

Baben—(m)—from grandfathers

Babig—(m)—grandfather

Badouagan—(m)—honourable

Badrig—(m)—noble

Baghdasar—(m)—wise

Baidzar—(f)—bright

Balthazar- wise one

Barbara—(f)—savage, wild

Barbi—(f)—traveller

Bared—(m)—marshal

Barig—(f)—fairy

Barije—(f)—kind, soft

Baris—(m)—bear

Barkev—(m)—gift

Barkev—(m)—gift, presence

Barkhoudar—(m)—lucky

Barooyr—(m)—circuit, ring, circle, name of a famous poet and author, radius, surrounding

Barsam—(m)—great fire

Barshamin—(m)—figure
Bartev—(m)—gigantic, tall
Baruyr—(m)—radius, surrounding
Barzig—(f)—plain
Bath—(m)—baal protect the king
Baydzar—(f)—clear, bright
Baykar—(m)—perseverence
Beatrice—(f)—kind, soft
Beatris—(f)—blessed traveller
Beatrix—(f)—bringer of joy
Bebo—(m)—loved one
Bedirhan—(m)—daring, winner
Bedros—(m)—stone
Bedrosian—(m)—descended from peter
Belphegor—(m)—daring, winner
Bendik—(m)—the blessed
Berdi—(m)—magnificent, splendid
Berdj—(m)—joyfull, elegant
Berdjouhi—(f)—joyfull, elegant lady
Berge—(m)—to help, magnificent, splendid
Berj—(f)—superb, abundant, luxurious
Berj—(m)—elegant, magnificent, splendid, superb, abundant, luxurious
Berjanoush—(f)—elegantly sweet
Berjouhi—(f)—elegant female, joyfull
Berjouhie—(f)—abundant, luxurious
Berk—(m)—bear
Bersin—(f)—kind, soft
Bettina—(f)—god has sworn
Bianca—(f)—white shining
Bienathatha—(f)—kind, soft
Birgit—(f)—bright one
Blondine—(f)—the blonde

Boghos—(m)—minor, small, humble
Boujemaa—(m)—daring, winner
Brigitte—(f)—high one, strength
Brisia—(f)—artistic woman
Brosh—(m)—lips
Brother—(m)—daring, winner
Bsag—(m)—crown

CHAPTER THREE

Armenian Baby Names—C

Candace—(m)—biblical name

Caprice—(f)—impulsive

Carennina—(f)—form of catherine

Carina—(f)—clean, pure

Carine—(f)—form of catherine, friend, pure, maiden

Carni—(f)—a village in the kotayk province of armenia known for the temple of garni

Carnie—(f)—a village in the kotayk province

Carnig—(m)—small lamb

Carol—(f)—female form of charles, manly

Caroline—(f)—female form of charles, manly, girl

Caroun—(f)—spring

Catherine—(f)—forever pure

Celia—(f)—heaven

Centina—(f)—victor

Chan—(m)—soul

Chanig—(m)—soul

Charents—(m)—grim

Charentz—(m)—naughty, mischievous

Charlotte—(f)—manly, tiny, feminine

Chato—(m)—flat nose

Cheenar—(f)—the plane tree

Chinar—(f)—the plane tree

Chiva—(f)—a village in armenia

Chiva—(m)—a village in armenia

Christapor—(m)—armenian version of christopher, christ-bearer

Christiane—(f)—anointed

Christina—(f)—anointed

Christoph—(m)—who holds christ in his heart

Christopher—(m)—bearing christ

Ciel—(f)—from heaven, heavenly

Cinnamon—(f)—the spice

Claire—(f)—bright, shiny, glossy

Claudia—(f)—lame

Claus—(m)—victor by the people, loved by all

Clemens—(m)—gentle

Cohar—(f)—jewel, gem

Concepcion—(f)—kind, soft

Constanze—(f)—steadfast

Corina—(f)—virgin

Cornelia—(f)—the horned

Cynthia—(f)—flowery

CHAPTER FOUR

ARMENIAN BABY NAMES—D

Dadour—(m)—gift of god

Dajad—(m)—gift

Dajana—(f)—god is reconciling

Dakaria—(f)—kind, soft

Dalal—(f)—modest, coquetry

Dalida—(f)—female, virgin

Dalina—(f)—noble

Dalita—(f)—female, virgin, pure

Dalita—(f)—virgin

Danay—(f)—kind, soft

Daniel—(m)—god is my judge

Daniela—(f)—god is my judge

Danijela—(f)—god is my judge

Daphna—(f)—victory

Dareh—(m)—wealthy one

Darlita—(f)—young

Daron—(m)—a province in Armenia, great, region in armanian

Datev—(f)—an armenian monastery, also spelled tatev

Datev—(m)—an armenian monastery, also spelled tatev, god give wings

Datevig—(f)—god gives small wings, pious, clear

Davigh—(f)—ancient armenian harp

Davit—(m)—great hero

Davros—(m)—gift from god

Decille—(f)—vision

Delsin—(m)—he is so

Demi—(f)—mythological goddess of corn and harvest

Denise—(f)—fertility

Derev—(f)—leaf

Dernig—(m)—from god

Deron—(m)—small but great, belongs to god

Dertad—(m)—king's name

Deshi—(m)—gold golden

Diana—(f)—goddess of the moon

Dickran—(m)—name of a king

Dicran—(m)—a great king of armenia

Diko—(f)—armenian emperor

Dikran—(m)—fighter with arrow, an ancient armenian emperor called tigran the great, name of a king

Dikranouhi—(f)—flower, queen, king's daughter

Dikranuhi—(f)—the feminine version of dikran, fighter with arrow, armenian emperor

Dimitrije—(m)—follower of demeter

Dinah—(f)—only daughter

Dion—(m)—fertility

Dir—(m)—mythological god of armenian letters, sciences, arts and eloquence

Diradour—(m)—given to the lord

Dirair—(m)—man of god

Diran—(m)—derived from god, dominant, owner

Dirayr—(m)—holy man

Dirouhi—(f)—flower, holy woman, princess, lady

Ditsuhi—(f)—divinity, goddess

Diva—(f)—divine one

Domenica—(f)—born on sunday, of the lord

Donabed—(m)—head of celebration

Donig—(m)—head of celebration

Doris—(f)—gift

Drtad—(m)—gift of god, king's name

Dunja—(f)—esteemed, fitness

Dunya—(f)—fitness, life on earth

Dursun—(m)—daring, winner

Dvin—(f)—the capital city of early Armenia, a village in armenia

Dzadour—(m)—male name

Dzaghganoush—(f)—sweet flower

Dzaghig—(f)—flower

Dzeroun—(m)—wise man

Dzia—(f)—short for dziadzan, rainbow

Dziadzan—(f)—rainbow

Dziran—(f)—apricot

Dzirani —(f)—color of apricot

Dzovag—(m)—lake, one with eyes the color of the sea

Dzovig—(f)—small ocean

Dzovik—(f)—small sea

Dzovinar—(f)—sea fire

CHAPTER FIVE

Armenian Baby Names—E

Eemasdouhi—(f)—wise lady

Eesahag—(m)—he laughs

Eeshkhan—(m)—prince

Eghtsanoush—(f)—wish+sweet

Egon—(m)—strong with a sword

Eitan—(m)—steady

Ekaterina—(f)—pure

Elaine—(f)—shining, light

Elena—(f)—shining light, bright one

Elfi—(f)—peace

Elfriede—(f)—devotee one

Elga—(f)—elfin spear

Eliana—(f)—the

Elian—(m)—light

Elias—(m)—christ is my god

Elisabeth—(f)—god has sworn

Elise—(f)—form of elizabeth

Elise—(f)—promise of god, god is my oath

Eliza—(f)—god has sworn

Eliz—(f)—form of elizabeth

Elke—(f)—of noble birth
Ella luna—(f)—kind, soft
Elliotte—(m)—daring, winner
Elmast—(f)—diamond
Elmas—(f)—like a diamond
Elmaz—(f)—like a diamond
Elmes—(f)—as a diamond
Elmez—(f)—resembling to diamond
Elmis—(f)—diamond
Elmiz—(f)—diamond like
Elora—(f)—god is my light
Elsa—(f)—god has sworn
Elu—(f)—beautiful, fair
Emanuel—(m)—god is with us
Emasdouhi—(f)—wise lady
Emilija—(f)—kind, soft
Emiliya—(f)—to strive, excel, rival
Emily—(f)—rival
Emin—(m)—trustworthy, confident, honest
Emirkan—(m)—daring, winner
Emmanouel—(m)—god is with us
Emma—(f)—industrious, all-containing
Emy—(f)—great, great
Endzanoush—(f)—sweet gift
Endza—(f)—gift
Erato—(f)—poetry, lovely, beloved
Erika—(f)—ruler of the law
Erik—(m)—ruler of the law
Erna—(f)—determination
Esaia—(m)—salvation of christ
Esgouhi—(f)—female real
Eshkhan—(m)—prince
Esra—(f)—help, helper

Eteri—(f)—pure as heaven

Eugene—(f)—from greek noble

Eunji—(m)—pretty successful in life

Euphemia—(f)—auspicious speech, good repute, well regarded

Euphrosina—(f)—joy

Evaluna—(f)—kind, soft

Evangelia—(f)—good tidings

Evangeline—(f)—well

Evangelista—(f)—kind, soft

Evanna—(f)—young fighter

Eva—(f)—life, living

Eveline—(f)—hazelnut

Evelin—(f)—shapely, clean

Ewald—(m)—powerful in the law

Eznik—(m)—great male name

CHAPTER SIX

Armenian Baby Names—F

Felix—(m)—happy

Femi—(f)—love

Fidal—(m)—faith

Fimi—(f)—place name, river name

Fini—(f)—complete

Finn—(m)—warrior

Fiorella—(f)—flower

Flora—(f)—bloom

Flora—(f)—flower

Florian—(m)—bloom

Fozia—(f)—kind, soft

Franciska—(f)—frenchman

Franklina—(f)—frenchman, speer

Fransiska—(f)—a frenchman

Franziska—(f)—free

Freddy—(m)—peaceful ruler

Fridolin—(m)—peace, protection

Friedegunde—(f)—peace, protection

Friedrich—(m)—merciful leader

CHAPTER SEVEN

Armenian Baby Names—G

Gabriela—(f)—god is with us

Gabriele—(f)—god given strength

Gaby—(f)—woman of god

Gacia—(f)—cinnamon, cinnamon tree

Gadar—(f)—peak, summit, pure

Gadara—(f)—from the top of a mountain

Gadarine—(f)—catherine, from the top of a mountain

Gagik—(m)—pious, clear, small cross, old armenian for cross

Gaia—(f)—short for gayane

Gaiane—(f)—christian maiden martyr, earth

Gaidar—(m)—active, vivacious

Gaidzag—(m)—lightning

Gakav—(f)—partridge

Gakavig—(f)—partridge, young partridge

Gali—(f)— female version of galoust, arrival

Gamo—(m)—from will

Gamsar—(m)—faulty peak

Garabed—(m)—forerunner, guide, fore-runner, outrider

Garbis—(m)—fruit, gary, spear

Garen—(m)—able, guardian, mighty with a spear

Garik—(m)—spear ruler

Garin—(f)—city in western armenia now called erzroom, guardian, mighty with a spear

Garine—(f)—an old city, ancient city, from the city of garin

Garlen—(m)—abbreviation of carl marx and lenin

Garni—(f)—the last remaining pagean temple in armenia

Garnig—(m)—small lamb

Garo—(m)—forerunner, guide, looming, desire, missing someone, fore-runner, outrider

Garod—(f)—longing

Garri—(m)—spear

Gars—(f)—ancient city

Gasia—(f)—cinnamon tree

Gateel—(f)—drop of water or rain drop

Gayane—(f)—a martyr, christian maiden martyr, earth, a 4th century armenian apostolic church

Gaydzag—(m)—lightning

Gdridg—(m)—brave

Gdridge—(m)—brave

Gdrij—(m)—brave, courageous

Geghanoush—(f)—elegant, lovely

Geghanush—(f)—sweet and nice

Geghush—(f)—sweet and nice

Georg—(m)—farmer or husbandman

George—(m)—editor of the earth, farmer

Gerd—(m)—strong with the spear

Gerda—(f)—strong with the spear

Gerhard—(m)—strong with the spear

Gerlise—(f)—kind, soft

Gevorg—(m)—pious, clear

Gevork—(m)—farmer

Gharib—(m)—alien, stranger, visitor, traveller

Ghazar—(m)—god has helped

Ghazaros—(m)—god has helped

Ghevont—(m)—lion

Ghougas—(m)—bright light

Ghoukas—(m)—form of luke

Ghoungyanos—(m)—bright light

Gibrianos—(m)—inhabitant

Giragos—(m)—state

Giunone—(f)—kind, soft

Gohar—(f)—precious gem

Gomidas—(m)—an armenian priest, musicologist, composer, arranger, having long hair

Gor—(m)—brave, proud, lion's cub

Gorandoukht—(f)—lion's female cub

Gorune—(m)—lion's cub

Goryoun—(m)—lion's cub

Gosdan—(m)—loyal

Gosdantia—(f)—constant

Gosdantin—(m)—loyal

Gosdantina—(f)—constant

Goulizar—(f)—golden flower

Goulnaz—(f)—flower

Grag—(f)—fire

Gumach—(f)—from arabic fabric

Gunther—(m)—battle army

Guregh—(m)—from greek, lord, ruler

Gurgen—(m)—pious, clear, son of lion

Gyula—(m)—the young man, dedicated to jupiter

CHAPTER EIGHT

Armenian Baby Names—H

Hagint—(f)—precious blue stone, a flower

Hagop—(m)—james, jacob, supplanter

Hagop—(m)—name of a saint, supplanter

Haig—(m)—Armenian, from the hedged enclosure, giant man

Haik—(m)—armenian

Hakob—(m)—pious, clear

Hamak—(m)—charming

Hamaspouyr—(f)—wide spread

Hamazasb—(m)—charming

Hamesd—(f)—modest female

Hamesdouhi—(f)—modest female

Hamik—(m)—charming

Hamo—(m)—charming

Hampartsoom—(m)—ascension of jesus

Hamparzoum—(m)—resurrection

Hampig—(m)—ascension of jesus

Hannah—(f)—grace of god

Hannahmarie—(f)—kind, soft

Hannes—(m)—christ is gracious

Hans—(m)—christ is gracious
Hapet—(m)—bibical name given to azariah
Hardtmuth—(m)—daring, winner
Haris—(m)—strong, safe, guarded
Haro—(m)—easter, resurrection of jesus
Harout—(m)—pious, clear, resurrection of jesus
Haroutioun—(m)—resurrection, easter
Haroutiun—(m)—resurrection of jesus
Haroutyoun—(m)—resurrection
Harut—(m)—pious, clear
Harutyun—(m)—easter, pious, clear
Hasmig—(f)—jasmine
Hasmik—(f)—flower's name, jasmine, smiling
Haverj—(f)—eternal
Hayarpi—(f)—armenian sunrise, sun
Hayasdan—(m)—armenia
Hayaser—(m)—someone who loves the armenian race
Hayastan—(f)—armenia
Hayg—(m)—armenian
Haygag—(m)—Armenian, eye
Hayganoush—(f)—sweet
Haygaram—(m)—noble armenian
Haygaz—(m)—related to the armenian identity
Haygazoun—(m)—related to the armenian identity
Haygouhi—(f)—female armenian
Hayk—(m)—legendary hero
Hayrabed—(m)—patriarch
Hayrig—(m)—father
Hayrik—(m)—father
Haytoug—(m)—a soldier in a revolutionary army
Hazar—(m)—a thousand
Hazarapet—(m)—head of a thousand soldiers
Heather—(f)—flowering evergreen plant

Heghine—(f)—basket full of beautiful roses, light
Heghineh—(f)—sun
Heghnar—(f)—deer
Helmut—(m)—courageous protector
Hera—(f)—female warrior or hero
Hera—(f)—queen of gods, protector, heroine, short for heranoush
Herand—(m)—unquenchable fire
Heranoush—(f)—fire, sweet, one with beautiful hair
Herbert—(m)—army
Hereknaz—(f)—stop being delicate
Heriknaz—(f)—stop being delicate
Hermine—(f)—daughter of hermes
Hermineh—(f)—daughter of hermes
Heros—(m)—hero
Hetoum—(m)—armenian king
Hiwa—(m)—signalling
Hmayag—(m)—charming
Hmayak—(m)—charming
Hnazant—(f)—obedient
Hnazant—(m)—obedient
Hoki—(m)—soul, spirit
Hoky—(m)—soul, spirit
Hooys—(f)—hope
Houdit—(f)—female jew
Hourher—(f)—flaming hair, red-headed
Houri—(f)—fairy, flames
Hourig—(f)—fairy-flames, little fire
Houshig—(f)—small memory
Housig—(m)—hope
Hovag—(m)—god rising, source of wind
Hovagim—(m)—god rising, source of wind
Hovan—(m)—god's gift

Hovasap—(m)—master judge

Hoven—(m)—from the wind, god's gift, god is gracious

Hovhaness—(m)—god's gift, god is gracious

Hovhannes—(m)—christ is merciful, gracious

Hovig—(m)—breeze, grace of god

Hovnan—(m)—dove

Hovnatan—(m)—god given

Hovsep—(m)—form of joseph, god will, god shall add

Hrach—(m)—pious, clear

Hrachya—(m)—pious, clear

Hrad—(m)—the planet mars, hot as fire

Hrag—(m)—fiery eyes, source of flames

Hrahad—(m)—fire grain, piece of fire

Hrair—(m)—man of fire

Hrant—(m)—name of a planet jupiter, unquenchable fire

Hrantouhi—(f)—female jupiter

Hrarpi—(f)—fire sun

Hratch—(m)—one with fiery eyes

Hratchia—(m)—one with fiery eyes

Hratchouhi—(f)—fire-eyed, fire-eyed female

Hravart—(m)—burning rose

Hrayr—(m)—man of flames

Hraztan—(m)—a river in Armenia, gun

Hreghen—(f)—fiery

Hripsime—(f)—a 7th century armenian apostolic church in Armenia, christian maiden martyr, prestigious

Hripsimeh—(f)—christian maiden martyr, prestigious

Hrout—(f)—friend

Hurensohn—(m)—daring, winner

Huseyin—(m)—well

CHAPTER NINE

Armenian Baby Names—I

Igor—(m)—warrior

Ilan—(m)—tree

Ilse—(f)—god has sworn

Imasdouhi—(f)—wise lady

Indrawan—(m)—daring, winner

Ingeborg—(f)—god

Ingmar—(m)—famous

Ingrid—(f)—god

Ionel—(m)—god is reconciling

Ipo—(m)—coming from frisian names

Irene—(f)—peace

Iris—(f)—river in armenian

Isabel—(f)—consecrated to god, god is perfection

Isabella—(f)—consecrated to god, god has sworn, god is perfection

Isgouhi—(f)—authentic woman, female real

Ishkhan—(m)—prince

Ismail—(m)—god will hear

Ivan—(m)—christ is gracious

Izmirlian—(m)—from izmir

CHAPTER TEN

Armenian Baby Names—J

Jan—(m)—soul

Jana—(f)—divine

Janig—(m)—soul, spirit

Janik—(m)—god is gracious

Jannig—(m)—dear, sweet

Jano—(m)—god is merciful, gracious

Jarbig—(m)—clever, able

Jasmin—(f)—jasmine blossom

Jason—(m)—mythological name

Jbdouhi—(f)—smiling

Jbdouhi—(f)—smiling lady

Jebid—(f)—smile

Jennifer—(f)—fruitful

Jesper—(m)—treasure holder

Jessica—(f)—flowery

Jew—(m)—the praise of the lord, confession

Jirair—(m)—active man, hard working

Jirayr—(m)—agile, hard-working

Jiro—(m)—active man

Jivan—(m)—youthful, life, energising, source of life

Johann—(m)—christ is gracious
Johanna—(f)—lord is gracious
Jolanda—(f)—violet flower
Jonas—(m)—dove
Jonathan—(m)—gift from god
Jorg—(m)—farmer
Josef—(m)—may the lord add
Joud—(f)—chickadee
Joudig—(f)—chickadee
Jovan—(m)—god is with us
Jrak—(f)—spark
Jud—(m)—praised
Julia—(f)—flower plant
Juliana—(f)—downy bearded, youthful
Justus—(m)—righteous

CHAPTER ELEVEN

Armenian Baby Names—K

Kach—(m)—brave

Kacher—(m)—many brave ones

Kachig—(m)—brave, young

Kaghtsrig—(m)—sweety

Kaghtzrig—(f)—sweetie

Kaghtzrig—(m)—sweety

Kai—(m)—key holder

Kail—(m)—wolf

Kakig—(m)—old armenian for cross

Kakig—(m)—small cross

Kale—(m)—walk

Kaloosh—(m)—blessed event

Kalousd—(m)—pentecost

Kaloust—(m)—pentecost

Kalusd—(m)—pentecost

Kamer—(m)—from arabic moon

Kami—(f)—strong wind

Kamraan—(m)—victorious

Kapriel—(m)—gabriel, strong man of god

Kapriel—(m)—strong man of god

Karayan—(m)—dark
Karekin—(m)—valuable, worth quadruple
Karine—(f)—form of karen, pure one
Karmo—(m)—from will
Karni—(f)—a good listener, temple, pagan temple
Karnig—(m)—lambkin, small lamb
Karoon—(f)—spring
Karoun—(f)—season of spring, spring
Karyan—(f)—the dark one
Kasbar—(m)—gemstone, priest
Katrin—(f)—clean and pure
Kay—(m)—key holder
Kayane—(f)—christian maiden martyr-earth
Kayl—(m)—wolf
Kazavon—(m)—armenian prince
Kegham—(m)—beauty, born in a good year, handsome
Keghani—(f)—pretty female
Keghanoush—(f)—elegant, lovely
Keghanoush—(f)—sweet and nice
Keghart—(m)—spear
Keghetsig—(f)—beautiful, very pretty, stunning
Keghetzig—(f)—beautiful
Keghon—(m)—glory, dedication
Keghouhi—(f)—fair, fair lady
Keghoun—(m)—handsome
Keghoush—(f)—sweet and nice
Kenel—(m)—to buy, purchase
Keran—(f)—wooden post, horn
Keren—(m)—a wooden post
Kero —(m)—angel, cherub
Kerop—(m)—angel, cherub
Kerovpe—(m)—angel, cherub
Kersam—(m)—foreigner

Kerstin—(f)—christian

Kesag—(m)—budget

Kevork—(m)—farmer, George, name of a saint

Khachadour—(m)—given by cross

Khacher—(m)—many crosses

Khachig—(m)—small cross

Khachik—(m)—small cross

Khacho—(m)—cross

Khajag—(m)—blue eyed

Khalaf—(m)—successor

Khatchadour—(m)—given to the cross

Khatcheres—(m)—cross-face

Khatchig—(m)—small cross

Khatchouhi—(f)—little cross, small cross

Khatoun—(f)—princess

Khigar—(m)—wise, clever

Khngeni—(f)—frankincense source

Khonarh—(f)—humble

Khoren—(m)—from the sun, pious, clear

Khorodig—(f)—sweet

Khosrov—(m)—an ancient armenian king, having a good name

Khosrovanoush—(f)—khosrov's sister

Khosrovitoukhd—(f)—princess name

Khoumar—(f)—from arabic drunk

Khoyan—(f)—rams

Kinevart—(f)—wine-coloured rose, wine-rose

Kion—(m)—daring, winner

Kirkan—(m)—vigilant, watchful

Kirkir—(m)—one who is vigilant, raising a sun

Klkhatir—(f)—put over the head

Knar—(f)—harp, lyre

Knarig—(f)—lyre

Knkoush—(f)—tender

Kohar—(f)—gem, jewel, precious gem

Koharig—(f)—jewel

Koko—(m)—awake

Kolb—(m)—pious, clear

Komitas—(m)—arranger, singer, who is considered the founder of the armenian national school of music

Konstantin—(m)—steady, stable

Korian—(m)—name of a historian

Kourken—(m)—son of lion

Kousan—(m)—singer

Krik—(m)—pious, clear

Krikor—(m)—awake, fast, form of gregory

Kristapor—(m)—christ bearer, the name of an armenian hero: kristapor mikaelian

Kud—(m)—discovery

Kurt—(m)—bold counsel, honest advisor

CHAPTER TWELVE

Armenian Baby Names—L

Lala—(f)—tulip, well spoken, giving respect

Lalig—(f)—tulip small

Laparoscopia—(m)—daring, winner

Lar—(f)—musical instrument strings

Lara—(f)—famous, well-known, cheerful, pleasant

Lareen—(f)—ancient armenian currency

Larine—(f)—ancient armenian currency

Laura—(f)—the laurel tree, honour, victory

Lavinia—(f)—evergreen

Lea—(f)—lion

Leem—(f)—an island in lake van in armenia

Lelag—(f)—lilac, violet color

Lena—(f)—charming woman, lion, hard, seductress

Leniya—(f)—seductress

Lennart—(m)—lion, hard

Lenz—(m)—from laurentum, italy

Leo—(m)—lion

Leonardo—(m)—lion, hard

Leonie—(f)—lion

Lernig—(m)—small mountain

Lernik—(m)—small mountain
Levi—(m)—attached, pledged
Levon—(m)—lion, joined, attached
Lewis—(m)—fame
Libarid—(m)—beloved
Lieselotte—(f)—dedicated to god
Lili—(f)—a flower, symbol for purity
Lilit—(f)—ghost, storm goddess
Lim—(f)—an island in lake van in armenia
Londa—(m)—daring, winner
Looys—(f)—light
Lor—(f)—quail
Lorand—(m)—famous
Loreni—(f)— linden tree
Lorenz—(m)—the award-winning
Lori—(f)—linden tree, the laurel tree, region in armenia
Lorie—(f)—city in armenia
Lorig—(f)—young quail
Lorik—(f)—quail
Loris—(m)—clown
Lory—(f)—linden tree
Louisa—(f)—light
Lous—(f)—light
Lousaper—(f)—abundance of light
Louseres—(f)—bright face
Lousig—(f)—small light
Lousin—(f)—moon
Lousine—(f)—moon
Lousineh—(f)—moon
Lousntak—(f)—crown of light
Lousvart—(f)—light rose
Louys—(m)—light
Luca—(m)—light

Lucine—(f)—moon, light
Lucy—(f)—bringer of light, light, form of light
Lukas—(m)—masculinity
Luseres—(f)—face with a bright and radiant glow
Lusine—(f)—moon
Lusineh—(f)—moon
Lyo—(m)—daring, winner

CHAPTER THIRTEEN

Armenian Baby Names—M

Madat—(m)—master's gift

Madlen—(f)—woman

Madlene—(f)—from a city

Madteos—(m)—gift of god

Magar—(m)—attendant, lucky

Maguy—(f)—pearl

Makrouhi—(f)—cleaner

Malkhas—(m)—quality

Mamigon—(m)—noble family

Mampre—(m)—rebel, insurgent

Manajihr—(m)—good mind

Manase—(m)—forgetting

Mane—(f)—weave

Maneh –derived from the word manana, semolina

Manfred—(m)—man of peace

Mangasar—(m)—head of children

Manish—(f)—violet

Manishag—(f)—violet flower

Manoug—(m)—child, infant

Manough—(m)—infant

Manoushag—(f)—violet
Manoush—(f)—devotee
Manuel—(m)—god is with us, powerful, strong
Manuela—(f)—god is with us
Manush—(f)—violet
Manushag—(f)—violet, the flower
Maral—(f)—beautiful, deer
Maralik—(f)—a town in armenia
Mardig—(m)—warrior
Mardiros—(m)—martyr
Mardoun—(m)—village
Mardouni—(m)—region and city in armenia
Marem—(f)—from mary
Margaid—(f)—pearl
Margaret—(f)—pearl
Margarete—(f)—pearl
Margo—(f)—from pearl
Margos—(m)—marcus, mark
Mari—(f)—rebellious woman, wished of child
Maria—(f)—bitter, pleasure of joy
Marie—(f)—bitter
Marine—(f)—christian maiden martyr
Marineh—(f)—christian maiden martyr
Mario—(m)—warring
Maritsa—(f)—form of maria
Marius—(m)—masculinity
Mariyam—(f)—pomegranate, wished for a child, love
Mark—(m)—god of war
Markar—(m)—prophet
Markrid—(f)—pearl, daisy
Markus—(m)—son of mars
Marmar—(f)—marble

Maro—(f)—bitter, myself
Marta—(f)—mistress
Martin—(m)—servant of mars, god of war
Martina—(f)—the little warrior
Martinus—(m)—dedicated to mars
Mashdots—(m)—ancient city
Masis—(m)—mount masis
Matas—(m)—daring, winner
Mateo—(m)—gift
Matous—(m)—god's present, gift of god
Matsag—(m)—male
Matthew—(m)—gift of god
Matthias—(m)—gift from god
Maximilian—(m)—little
Mayda—(f)—kind, maiden
Mayis—(m)—the month of may
Mayranoush—(f)—sweet mother
Medaks—(f)—silk
Medaksya—(f)—made of silk
Medax—(f)—silky
Megheti—(f)—melody
Meghety—(f)—melody
Meghranoush—(f)—honey-sweet
Meghri—(f)—a region in armenia, honey
Meghrig—(m)—honey
Meinrad—(m)—strong
Mekhag—(f)—carnation, cloves
Mekhag—(m)—clove
Melanie—(f)—black, dark in colour
Melik—(m)—prince, king
Melineh—(f)—sweet, honey
Melissa—(f)—bee
Melkon—(m)—prince

Melvin—(m)—friend

Merian—(f)—shapely clean

Meroujan—(m)—sunny soul

Mesrob—(m)—clerk, inventor of the armenian alphabet

Mesrop—(m)—name of a saint

Mgerditch—(m)—baptist

Mgrditch—(m)—baptist, a religious person

Mgrdoum—(m)—baptism

Mher—(m)—love, impress, name of an armenian hero

Michael—(m)—like god, popular

Michaela—(f)—who is likes god

Mierda—(m)—daring, winner

Mihr—(m)—angel of friendship, grants

Mihran—(m)—skilled

Mihrtad—(m)—gift of god

Mikael—(m)—like god

Mina—(f)—love, will, desire, helmet

Minas—(m)—month, tower, the great one

Miriam—(f)—rebellious woman

Mirna—(f)—beloved

Misak—(m)—agreement

Misho—(m)—pious, clear

Missak—(m)—agreement

Mjej—(m)—prince

Mkhitar—(m)—comforter

Mleh—(m)—king

Mnatsagan—(m)—permanent, eternal

Momig—(m)—small candle

Monika—(f)—attractive bird

Mourad—(m)—wish

Mouron—(m)—holy oil

Moush—(m)—an ancient armenian city, city in old armenia

Moushe—(m)—city in old armenia
Moushegh—(m)—taken from god
Movses—(m)—deliver, moses, saved from the water

CHAPTER FOURTEEN

ARMENIAN BABY NAMES—N

Nadalia—(f)—born on christmas

Nadine—(f)—hope

Nadja—(f)—hope

Nael—(m)—daring, winner

Nahabed—(m)—patriarch

Naire—(f)—land of rivers

Nairi—(f)—from a canyon land, kind one

Nane—(f)—god has favoured me, nice, goddess of war

Nanor—(f)—new baby

Nanor—(f)—sleep, lullaby

Nar—(m)—tears of blood

Nara—(m)—flower of pomegranate

Nare—(f)—from nar, symbolic fruit

Nareg—(m)—ancient city, well-sharpened sword, ancient city

Nareh—(f)—color of pomegranate

Narek—(m)—book

Nargiz—(f)—narcissus, narcissus flower

Narin—(f)—the part of the branch of the pomegranate tree that has the fruit and flowers

Narineh—(f)—from a city

Narod—(f)—the crown in the armenian wedding crowning ceremony

Nartos—(m)—lavender

Nartouhi—(f)—feminine lavender

Nashkhoun—(f)—decorated, lovely

Natalie—(f)—birthday, given

Natan—(m)—god given

Natel—(f)—christmas

Nathalie—(f)—birthday

Nathaniel—(m)—god has given

Navasart—(m)—armenian new year, name of month

Nayat—(f)—flow

Nayiri—(f)—historically, the land of canyons or river,old name for armenian lands, the land of canyons or river

Nayirouhi—(f)—female nayiri

Nayree—(f)—old name for armenian lands

Nayree—(m)—old name for armenian lands

Naz—(f)—graceful

Nazani—(f)—delicate, graceful

Nazar—(m)—eyesight, vision, from nazareth, nazareth, childhood home of jesus

Nazaret—(m)—nazareth, childhood home of jesus, town named for nazareth

Nazeli—(f)—graceful

Nazeli—(f)—pretty

Nazely—(f)—graceful

Nazenig—(f)—graceful

Nazig—(f)—graceful

Nbad—(m)—the 26th day of an armenian month

Nectar—(f)—nectar

Negdar—(f)—nectar

Nerses—(m)—new hero
Neuvart—(f)—new rose
Nevart—(f)—new rose
Neyhal—(m)—daring, winner
Niclas—(m)—victory
Nico—(m)—conqueror of the people
Nicolas—(m)—victor by the people, loved by all
Nicole—(f)—conqueror of the people
Nigoghos—(m)—victory of the people
Nigol—(m)—conquerer of the people, new one
Nikolas—(m)—victory
Nina—(f)—the ever pure, pure
Nishan—(f)—award, medal
Nishan—(m)—miracles, symbol, signature, mark
Nishon—(m)—sign
Njteh—(m)—exile, foreigner, pilgrim, emigrant
Noahjesse—(m)—daring, winner
Noji—(f)—tree
Noor—(f)—pomegranate
Nora—(f)—new
Norayr—(m)—new male, new man
Norbert—(m)—splendour
Norendza—(f)—new gift
Norhad—(m)—new grain
Norris—(m)—caretaker, nurse
Norvan—(m)—new monastery
Noubar—(m)—fresh fruit
Noune—(f)—holy and pure
Nourhan—(m)—light+ han
Nouritsa—(f)—persian bright gold
Noushig—(f)—little almond
Nouvart—(f)—new rose
Nouver—(f)—gift, present

Noy—(m)—noah, rest, comfort
Noyemi—(f)—pleasant
Nshan—(m)—mark, sign, holycross
Nuneh—(f)—clean, holy
Nunuphar—(f)—a water flower, lily
Nvart—(f)—newly blossomed rose
Nver—(f)—gift
Nyshan—(m)—sign

CHAPTER FIFTEEN

Armenian Baby Names—O

Oda—(m)—greek ode, song, poem

Ohan—(m)—chief, god is gracious

Ohanna—(f)—god's gracious gift

Oksen—(m)—hospitable

Onnig—(m)—short form of john

Orig—(f)—day

Oror—(f)—lullaby

Osanna—(f)—hosanna

Oshagana—(m)—village in armenia

Oshakan—(m)—name of the village in armenia

Oshin—(m)—flower

Osig—(f)—benediction, praise

Oskie—(f)—gold

Otmar—(m)—by his inheritance, famous

Ovsan—(f)—benediction, praise

Ovsanna—(f)—benediction, praise

CHAPTER SIXTEEN

ARMENIAN BABY NAMES—P

Pagour—(m)—early

Pailag—(m)—lightning

Pailoon—(f)—shines brightly

Pakrad—(m)—god given

Pakradouhi—(f)—female of pakrat

Palasan—(f)—balsam

Paleni—(f)—cherry

Palig—(m)—child

Panig—(m)—all holy

Panos—(m)—lighthouse, rock, all holy

Papken—(m)—father's youngest son

Paramaz—(m)—son of the people

Parantsem—(f)—old persian silk

Parantzem—(f)—old persian silk

Pardi—(f)—tree

Pareen—(f)—femine for kind or good natured

Pareli—(f)—embraceable, lovely

Paren—(m)—from good

Pari—(f)—kind

Parig—(f)—fairy

Parik—(f)—kindness
Parin—(f)—femine for kind or good natured
Parkhoutar—(m)—lucky
Parnag—(m)—clear eyes
Parouhi—(f)—good
Parounag—(m)—grape vine
Parounak—(m)—thanks to god
Parsegh—(m)—lisping, stammering
Partogh—(m)—bartholomew
Partoghomeos—(m)—bartholomew
Patil—(f)—snow flake
Patrick—(m)—nobleman
Paul—(m)—small or modest
Pavagan—(f)—enough
Payl—(f)—shiny
Payla—(f)—short for pailadzou, planet of mercury
Paylag—(m)—lightning
Paze—(f)—falcon
Pega—(f)—delight
Pegor—(f)—piece, fragment
Peklar—(m)—ruler
Pelibbos—(m)—friend of horses
Penyamin—(m)—son of the south
Pergri—(f)—short for pergrouhie, delight
Pergrouhi—(f)—cheerful female
Peri—(f)—fairy
Perooz—(f)—turquoise
Perouz—(f)—precious stone
Perouze—(f)—turquoise
Persape—(f)—source of songs
Pertag—(m)—small castle
Peter—(m)—rock
Petra—(f)—rock

Philip—(m)—horses friend
Philipp—(m)—horses friend
Phineas—(m)—oracle
Phir—(m)—one who burns brightly
Phyre—(f)—burning bright
Phyre—(m)—burning bright
Pia—(f)—pious
Piera—(f)—small rock
Porcodio—(m)—daring, winner
Pounig—(f)—phoenix bird
Pouragn—(f)—of many sources
Pourasdan—(f)—flower garden
Pouregh—(f)—crystal
Pouzant—(m)—historian
Purad—(m)—gale
Puzant—(m)—historian

CHAPTER SEVENTEEN

Armenian Baby Names—R

Raffi—(m)—flash of lightning, glorious man, holding high, exalted

Rafi—(m)—comforter, form of raphael

Rahel—(f)—lamb, one with purity

Raied—(m)—daring, winner

Ralph—(m)—wolf

Ramiar—(m)—daring, winner

Raphael—(m)—god has healed, healed by god

Raphael—(m)—healed by god

Raqel—(f)—lamb, one with purity

Rashid—(m)—rightly guided

Rauno—(m)—daring, winner

Razmig—(m)—soldier, combatant, warrior, fighter

Razmik—(m)—fighter, sunlight

Razmouhi—(f)—fighter, fighter female

Regina—(f)—queen

Rehan—(f)—basil, flower, scented

Rehan—(m)—scented

Rene—(m)—reborn

Renzo—(m)—masculinity

Repega—(f)—tie
Reteos—(m)—prince
Rhythm—(m)—music, in-sequence
Ricci—(m)—curly haired
Rita—(f)—pearl, child of light
Robb—(m)—bright, shining
Robert—(m)—bright with glory
Robrecht—(m)—beautifully by fame
Roland—(m)—brave, brave
Roman—(m)—a citizen of rome
Romen—(m)—man from rome
Ronald—(m)—guides, ruler
Rosdom—(m)—mighty hero
Rouben—(m)—winner, lucky
Rouzan—(f)—from the name of an old armenian city
Rozin—(f)—from rose
Rshdouni—(m)—an ancient armenian dynasty
Rubina—(f)—the red gemstone, red, ruby
Rupen—(m)—lord of the form, ruby
Ruperta—(f)—beautifully by fame
Rupina—(f)—ruby female
Rurik—(m)—famous ruler
Ryan—(m)—kingly

CHAPTER EIGHTEEN

Armenian Baby Names—S

Saara—(f)—good, best star, nobel princess

Sabina—(f)—woman

Sabine—(f)—female name

Sabrina—(f)—legendary princess

Sahag—(m)—he who laughs, Armenian, the first name of the creator of the armenian alphabet

Sahaganoush—(f)—daughter

Said—(m)—happy

Sako—(m)—rainbow

Salpi—(f)—bird, cypress tree

Sami—(m)—exalted

Samson—(m)—bright as the sun, sun child, of the sun

Samuel—(m)—asked of god, told by god, god has heard

Samvel—(m)—asked of god, god has heard

Sanahin—(f)—name of an armenian monastery

Sanam—(f)—beloved, idol

Sanan—(f)—spear, gad

Sanasar—(m)—sacred mountain

Sanatroug—(m)—princess

Santoukhd—(f)—early christian, virgin

Sanyu—(m)—happiness
Sara—(f)—princess, queen, pure, lady
Sarah—(f)—princess
Saren– from the mountain
Sargis—(m)—pious, clear
Sarhad—(m)—border
Sarig—(f)—small mountain
Sarin—(f)—the best rose (of mountain)
Sarine—(f)—the best rose (of mountain)
Sarkis—(m)—protector, shepherd, rainbow
Sarmen—(m)—mix of sarkis and armen
Saro—(m)—cypress tree, mountaineer
Sasoun—(m)—an armenian province and city
Sassoun—(m)—joy
Saten—(f)—amber
Satenig—(f)—amber
Satin—(f)—amber
Sayat—(m)—the first name of the famous armenian poet and musician sayat nova
Sebastian—(m)—masculinity
Sebouh—(m)—knight, nobleman, nobleman, knight
Seda—(f)—echo's in the forest, voice, forest spirit, silk
Sedan—(f)—echo through the woods
Seida—(f)—echo through the woods
Selma—(f)—arabic peaceful, healthy
Selmon—(m)—daring, winner
Semag—(m)—seventh in the family
Sempad—(m)—victor
Ser—(f)—love
Serban—(m)—boy
Serig—(f)—love
Serik—(f)—love
Serine—(f)—love

Serj—(m)—god's servant, form of sarkis

Serli—(f)—full of love

Serly—(f)—full of love

Sero—(m)—love

Serop—(m)—fiery ones, to burn, group of angels, name of an armenian hero

Serouj—(m)—strength of love

Serovpe—(m)—fiery ones, to burn

Serpouhi—(f)—saintly

Serpuhi—(f)—holy

Set—(m)—appointed, compensation

Seta—(f)—forest spirit, silk

Setrag—(m)—god is my justice

Sevag—(m)—one with black eyes

Sevan—(f)—famous lake in armenia, the daughter of a famous armenian artist, from a lake

Sevana—(f)—related to lake sevan

Sevatch—(f)—one with black eyes

Sevoug—(f)—black, blacky

Shabouh—(m)—ancient armenian king's name

Shadarev—(m)—one who sees many suns -one who lives long

Shaghig—(f)—light rain

Shahan—(m)—belonging to a king, profit maker, falcon, king of kings

Shahanig—(f)—falcon

Shahe—(m)—falcon, to win

Shahen—(m)—falcon

Shakar—(f)—sugar

Shake—(f)—to let light in

Shamiram—(f)—queen

Shant—(m)—gentle, peace, calm, lightning

Sharar—(m)—navel thought, singing

Sharik—(m)—child of god

Sharmagh—(f)—fine sieve

Shavasb—(m)—black horse

Shemavon—(m)—god has heard

Shen—(m)—joyful, cheerful

Shin—(m)—real, true

Shirag—(m)—a village and province in armenia

Shirak—(m)—a village and province in armenia

Shiraz—(m)—sweet, the last name of an armenian poet, free as a lion

Shnorhig—(f)—graceful

Shnorhk—(m)—grace

Shogha—(f)—splendour

Shoghagat—(f)—splendour

Shogher—(f)—rays

Shogher—(f)—sunrays

Shoghig—(f)—small ray

Shoushan—(f)—white lily

Shoushanig—(f)—white lily

Shoushanik—(f)—flower's name

Shoushi—(f)—city in artsakh

Shoushig—(m)—white lily

Shushan—(f)—the flower lily

Shushi—(f)—a city in artsakh

Shushig—(f)—the flower lily

Siamanto—(m)—the pen name of a famous armenian writer

Sibyl—(f)—path, prophetess, seer, oracle

Sida—(f)—echo through the woods

Silke—(f)—win

Silva—(f)—forest, garden, vineyard

Silvia—(f)—of the forest

Silviu—(m)—forest or woods

Sima—(f)—sky, heaven, border, limit, boundary, symbol

Simon—(m)—god has heard, listening intently

Simona—(f)—god has heard

Sina—(f)— peacock

Sinam—(f)— peacock

Sinan—(m)—spear, gad

Sion—(m)—excellent, hill, god is merciful, highest point

Sipan—(m)—mountain in armenia

Sira—(f)—from love

Sirak—(m)—famous author, william saroyan's pen name, eyes full of love, source of love

Siran—(f)—beautiful, lovely

Siran—(f)—sweet love

Siranoush—(f)—a lovely woman, sweet love

Sirarpi—(f)—love of the sun, lovely daughter

Sirekan—(m)—lover

Sireli—(f)—dear

Siroon—(f)—pretty, lovely

Sirouhi—(f)—sweetheart, darling

Siroun—(f)—lovely

Sirov—(f)—with love

Sirpuhi—(f)—holy

Sirvart—(f)—rose of love

Sirvat—(f)—beautiful rose

Sis—(f)—a town in the ararat province of Armenia, mountain in armenia

Sisag—(m)—your joy

Smpad—(m)—victor

Soffi—(f)—wisdom

Soffiya—(f)—from greek wisdom

Soghome—(f)—aramaic peace

Soghomon—(m)—solomon, peace

Sograd—(m)—preserving power

Sona—(f)— a tall woman, gold, beautiful, pretty, precious, slender

Sophia—(f)—queen

Sos—(m)—bear, tree

Soseh—(f)—planetree

Sosi—(f)—planetree

Sosse—(f)—plane tree, armenian freedom fighter

Sossi—(f)—plane tree

Sossy—(f)—the plane tree

Sosy—(f)—planetree

Soukias—(m)—peaceful

Souren—(m)—of the sun, warlord

Srabion—(m)—fiery ones, to burn

Srpoug—(f)—female saint

Srpouhi—(f)—female saint

Stefan—(m)—crown wreath

Steiner—(m)—son

Stephan—(m)—crown

Stephanie—(f)—a crown of garland, crown, wreath

Suineh—(f)—a mountain in armenia

Suren—(m)—lord indra

Susanne—(f)—lily flower

Sussan—(f)—a flower, lily, lily of the valley, lotus flower

Suzaan—(f)—lily

Suzan—(f)—lily

Sweet—(f)—sweet

Sybilla—(f)—christ, prophetess, oracle

Sylva—(f)—love and rose, woods, woodland, forest

CHAPTER NINETEEN

ARMENIAN BABY NAMES—T

Takouhi—(f)—queen

Takoush—(f)—queen

Takuhi—(f)—queen

Takush—(f)—queen

Takvor—(m)—crowned

Talar—(f)—evergreen, fresh, green

Taleen—(f)—taline, talyn

Tali—(f)—diminutive of talar

Talin—(f)—a town in Armenia, unclear

Taline—(f)—city, monastery

Tamar—(f)—island and province in Armenia, palm tree, date palm

Tamara—(f)—palm tree

Tancred—(m)—thoughtful counsel

Tangakin—(f)—precious, valuable

Tania—(f)—father's daughter, daring

Taniel—(m)—god is my judge, judgement

Tarik—(m)—evening caller

Tarouhi—(f)—from persian soul

Tateos—(m)—praising god

Tatev—(f)—a village in armenia
Tatevik—(f)—to give a wing
Tatoul—(m)—skillful, good hands
Tavit—(m)—beloved
Tavtag—(m)—beloved
Tavush—(m)—one of the provinces in armenia
Teghtsanig—(f)—canary bird
Teghtsoun—(f)—blond, fair
Teotig—(m)—given to god
Terenig—(m)—monastery attendant
Teter—(f)—butterfly
Tevan—(m)—deity, prefix te plus kevin
Tevin—(f)—city in armenia
Theodora—(f)—god's present, gift of god
Theoxaris—(m)—daring, winner
Theresa—(f)—woman working at harvest
Thomas—(m)—twin
Thomas—(m)—twin, master of air bending
Thorin—(m)—thunder
Tiana—(f)—bird like
Tibor—(m)—the
Tigran—(m)—fighter with arrow, an ancient armenian emperor called tigran the great, shooting an arrow
Tim—(m)—shining
Timo—(m)—who honours god
Timotei—(m)—daring, winner
Timothy—(m)—one who honours god
Timun—(m)—god fearing
Tina—(f)—god has sworn
Tiridates—(m)—a king
Titer—(f)—butterfly
Tobias—(m)—god is my good

Torkom—(m)—armenian progenitor hayk's father, fore-ancestor of Armenians, bony

Tornig—(m)—grandson

Toros—(m)—gift from god

Toukhtzam—(f)—brunette, brown-haired

Trasdamard—(m)—continuing on one path without distraction

Tro—(m)—pious, clear, short name, straight walker, the name of an armenian hero

Troi—(m)—soldier

Tsakig—(m)—youngster

Tsangali—(f)—desirable

Tsdrig—(f)—daughter

Tshoghig—(f)—fine dew, reflection

Tsolag—(m)—source of glare

Tsoler—(f)—fine dew, glares, reflection

Tsolig—(f)—reflection

Tsoline—(f)—fine dew, glare, reflection

Tsouig—(f)—butterfly

Tsvig—(f)—seed

Tudor—(m)—warrior

Tvin—(m)—ancient capital of armenia

Tzavag—(m)—full of pain

CHAPTER TWENTY

Armenian Baby Names—U

Udo—(m)—heritage

CHAPTER TWENTY-ONE

Armenian Baby Names—V

Vache—(m)—nomadic cart

Vaghars—(m)—king's name

Vagharshag—(m)—king's name, brown bear

Vaghenag—(m)—the best

Vahagk—(m)—god of war and victory in armenian mythology

Vahagn—(m)—king of honesty

Vahakn—(m)—armenian god, god of war and victory in armenian mythology

Vahan—(m)—shield

Vahe—(m)—best, shield, strong

Vahi—(m)—one who is strong

Vahram—(m)—fast moving tiger, pious, clear

Vahrij—(m)—fast stream

Vakhtank—(m)—wolf bodied

Valeriu—(m)—strength, bravery

Van—(f)— city and lake in ancient armenia

Vana—(f)— city and lake in ancient Armenia, referring to van

Vanadour—(m)—host, inn-keeper

Vanagan—(m)—monk

Vanant—(m)—armenian prince

Vaneh—(f)—of crystal

Vaneni—(f)—of crystal

Vanessa—(f)—butterfly

Vanig—(m)—small town

Vanouhi—(f)—female from van city

Vanoush—(f)—sweet

Vanuhi—(f)—woman from the city of van

Vanya—(f)—made of crystal

Varak—(m)—29th day of the armenian month, name of a mountain range and monastary in armenia

Varant—(m)—city in artsakh

Varaztad—(m)—gift of heaven

Varnaz—(m)—victor

Varouj—(m)—male dove, strong

Varoujan—(m)—male bird of prey, male dove

Varseh—(f)—woman with beautiful hair

Varsenig—(f)—woman with beautiful hair

Vart—(m)—rose

Vartan—(m)—a famous armenian hero, giver of rose, rose giver

Vartanoush—(f)—sweet as a rose

Vartavar—(m)—a holiday in armenian church, transfiguration of christ

Varteni—(f)—rose bush

Vartenie—(f)—rose tree

Varter—(f)— bouquet of roses

Varteres—(m)—rose-face

Vartin—(m)—rose

Vartishah—(f)—rose king

Vartiter—(f)—rose and butterfly

Vartivar—(f)—transfiguration of christ

Vartivar—(m)—transfiguration of christ

Vartkes—(m)—hair like rose, one with rose colored and full hair

Vartoug—(f)—rose

Vartoughi—(f)—rose

Vartouhi—(f)—beautiful as a rose, rose lady

Vartoush—(f)—rose

Vartuhi—(f)—rose

Varty—(f)—rosy

Varvara—(f)—foreign woman

Varvare—(f)—foreign woman

Vasag—(m)—treacherous-person

Vasbourag—(m)—from a city

Vatche—(m)—nomadic cart, young boy

Vaughn—(m)—name of a city and lake in western armenia

Vayk—(m)—a town in armenia

Vazgen—(m)—pious, clear

Vazkanoush—(f)—daughter

Vazken—(m)—descendant of king

Vazrig—(m)—armenian prince

Vehanoush—(f)—noble and sweet

Vehantsnouhi—(f)—female nobless

Vehig—(f)—majestic, noble

Vem—(m)—boulder, stone

Vera—(f)—form of veronica

Verena—(f)—saintly

Verjin—(f)—armenian form of virgin

Verkine—(f)—armenian form of virgin

Veronika—(f)—victory

Vertchalous—(f)—twilight

Victor—(m)—victor

Victorian—(m)—winner

Vigen—(m)—victory

Viken—(m)—victor, victorious

Viktor—(m)—victor

Vilen—(m)—prince

Vishab—(m)—dragon

Vivien—(f)—lively, full of life

Vojo—(m)—daring, winner

Vosdan—(m)—capital city, the medieval armenian royal residence on lake van

Vosdanig—(m)—nobleman

Vosgan—(m)—form of gold

Vosgedzam—(f)—golden hair

Vosgee—(f)—gold

Vosgehad—(f)—gold seeds

Vosgemad—(f)—gold+finger

Vosgetel—(f)—golden thread

Vosgi—(m)—gold

Voshkie—(f)—golden

Voskan—(m)—golden

Voskie—(f)—gold

Vram—(m)—a derivative of an ancient armenian king's name, fiery

Vramshabouh—(m)—king's name

Vrej—(m)—revenge, vengeance

Vrejouhi—(f)—vengeance-female

Vrtanes—(m)—old name

Vruyr—(m)—armenian prince

Vyke—(m)—a town in armenia

CHAPTER TWENTY-TWO

ARMENIAN BABY NAMES—W

Walter—(m)—ruler of the army

Weizi—(m)—daring, winner

Wico—(m)—daring, winner

Winalt—(m)—friend

Wolfgang—(m)—advancing wolf

CHAPTER TWENTY-THREE

ARMENIAN BABY NAMES—Y

Yar—(f)—sweetheart

Yeghia—(m)—my god is the lord

Yeghiazar—(m)—my god is the lord

Yeghig—(m)—form of elias

Yeghisapet—(f)—my god is an oath

Yeghisheh—(m)—armenian philosopher

Yeghnig—(f)—hind, red deer

Yeghnik—(m)—deer, hind

Yeghsan—(f)—god is perfection

Yeghya—(m)—god is my god

Yeprad—(m)—a river in armenia

Yeprem—(m)—fruitful

Yeprouhi—(f)—fruitful-female

Yeram—(m)—flock of birds

Yeran—(f)—lucky

Yeran—(f)—lucky, blessed

Yerani—(f)—lucky, blessed

Yeranos—(m)—lucky

Yeranuhi—(f)—lucky

Yeraz—(f)—dream

Yerazig—(f)—dream-small
Yerchanig—(f)—happy
Yerchanig—(m)—happy, joyous
Yerevan—(m)—capital of armenia
Yergat—(m)—iron
Yerimya—(m)—god appointed
Yerneg—(f)—blessed
Yervant—(m)—an armenian king, fast
Yesayi—(m)—lord is salvation
Yester—(f)—esther, hester persian star
Yeter—(f)—adequate, ether- enough
Yetvart—(m)—rich guard
Yeva—(f)—eve, life-enhancing, alive, living
Yevkineh—(f)—wellborn, noble, honourable
Yevnige—(f)—honourable
Yezegiel—(m)—god gives strength
Yeznig—(m)—name of a philosopher
Yezras—(m)—help
Yezrig—(m)—edge
Yoichi—(m)—daring, winner
Yranig—(f)—blessed
Yubi—(m)—daring, winner

CHAPTER TWENTY-FOUR

Armenian Baby Names—Z

Zabel—(f)—god is my oath, god is perfection, the name of an ancient armenian queen

Zada—(f)—lucky one, fortunate, prosperous

Zadig—(m)—easter, born on easter

Zagir—(f)—flower

Zagiri—(f)—flower

Zahal—(m)—joy

Zakaria—(m)—god has remembered

Zakariya—(m)—zechariah, remembering god

Zanazan—(f)—various

Zapel—(f)—god is perfection

Zareh—(m)—protector, weeping, in pain

Zarmantoukht—(f)—amazing daughter

Zarmayr—(m)—amazing man

Zarmig—(m)—niece or nephew

Zarmineh—(f)—niece

Zarmouhi—(f)—niece

Zaroug—(f)—golden

Zarouhi—(f)—golden, princess, wonderful, amazing lady

Zartar—(f)—ornament

Zarvart—(f)—amazing rose

Zarzant—(m)—scary

Zatik—(m)—easter

Zaven—(m)—assistant

Zepour—(f)—breeze

Zepure—(f)—breeze

Zeroun—(m)—wise, sacrifice, respected

Ziazan—(f)—rainbow

Zlatko—(m)—gold

Zmroukhd—(f)—emerald

Zohrab—(m)—pious, clear, ruby

Zohrag—(m)—ruby gem

Zorair—(m)—strong man

Zoravar—(m)—army leader, powerful

Zoulal—(f)—pure, clear

Zvart—(f)—happy, joyous

****

****

Printed by Libri Plureos GmbH in Hamburg,
Germany